Laws That Changed History

Key Civil Rights Laws

Cavendish Square
New York

Kathryn Ohnaka

Published in 2020 by Cavendish Square Publishing, LLC

243 5th Avenue, Suite 136, New York, NY 10016

First Edition

Cataloging-in-Publication Data

Names: Ohnaka, Kathryn.
Title: Key civil rights laws / Kathryn Ohnaka.
Description: New York : Cavendish Square Publishing, 2020. | Series: Laws that changed history | Includes glossary and index.
Identifiers: ISBN 9781502655202 (pbk.) | ISBN 9781502655219 (library bound) | ISBN 9781502655226 (ebook)
Subjects: LCSH: Civil rights--United States--Juvenile literature.
Classification: LCC KF4750.O36 2020 | DDC 342.7308--dc23

Printed in the United States of America

Photo Credits: Cover, p. 1 Joseph Sohm/Shutterstock.com; p. 7 Brooks Kraft/Corbis Historical/Getty Images; pp. 8–9 Bob Parent/Archive Photos/Getty Images; pp. 12–13 Mario Tama/Getty Images; pp. 15, 24–25 AFP/Getty Images; p. 18 Rick Diamond/Getty Images; p. 19 Fotosearch/Archive Photos/Getty Images; p. 22 Universal Images Group/Getty Images; p. 29 Historical Picture Archive/Corbis Historical/Getty Images; pp. 30–31 David McNew/Getty Images; p. 33 Buyenlarge/Archive Photos/Getty Images; pp. 35, 46 © AP Images; pp. 39, 44 Bettmann/Getty Images; pp. 40–41 Underwood Archives/Archive Photos/Getty Images; p. 49 Steve Liss/The LIFE Images Collection/Getty Images; pp. 50–51 Stan Honda/AFP/Getty Images; p. 53 B Christopher/Alamy Stock Photo; p. 55 The Washington Post/Getty Images; p. 59 Kristi Blokhin/Shutterstock.com; p. 60 CalypsoArt/Shutterstock.com; p. 63 Pacific Press/Alamy Stock Photo; p. 64 Diego G Diaz/Shutterstock.com; cover and interior pages (capitol dome graphic) Alexkava/Shutterstock.com.

CONTENTS

Introduction

Look around you. Think about your classroom, your job, your neighborhood, your friends, and the people who live in your community. Think about the different origins, races, genders, and identities of those people. How many are different from you? How are they different? We have such diversity in our communities now, but if you had lived 100 years ago, your community would have looked very different.

Discrimination is the refusal of equal rights to someone based on their race, gender, immigration status, or sexual or gender identity. Not so long ago in America's history, people of color, women, Native Americans, and people of different gender identities and sexual orientations were not given the same rights as their white male counterparts. Throughout history, people of color have faced slavery, loss of land and property, lack of a voice in the government, and lack of jobs, and they have been refused entry to places such as restaurants and schools. In the past, women and people of color couldn't vote. Native Americans lost their land, and they still fight for it and their voting rights today. Before the 1960s, black people could not use the same facilities, such as schools, restaurants, and pools, as white people. In recent years, gay people have fought for their rights to be married and have the same health care as heterosexual people. Most recently, transgender people have been fighting for the right to access the bathroom that matches their identity and to participate in the same jobs as cisgender people, such as serving in the military. Think about your community now. Who faces discrimination? Is it over, or do we still have work to do?

Much of our history has been spent arguing about whose voice counts in our society. From voting and job opportunities to even sharing the same facilities, the battle for civil rights has been a long one. It took time, protests, court hearings, and arguments within the government to create the laws that protect our citizens today. However, the fight isn't over; groups still fight for the rights to vote, to own land, and to have the same jobs and protections as others. This book will discuss the key laws in the fight for civil rights that grant equality to America's citizens, and it will consider the struggles that still exist today.

Think about your life now. Do you have everything you need? Do you have a voice in your society, the ability to make your own career and medical choices, and the right to be with the person you love? How bad would your life have to be for you to face violence or prison, endure hunger strikes, walk across the country, or take over a prison to draw attention to your needs? How far would you go to ensure equality for yourself, your family, and your friends?

Now think about the people around you. What did they fight for? What do they fight for today? Are they equal?

Chapter 1

America's Early Days: Who Had Rights?

In 1776, the Declaration of Independence declared, "We hold these Truths to be self-evident, that all Men are created equal, that they are endowed by their Creator with certain unalienable Rights, that among these are Life, Liberty, and the Pursuit of Happiness." These iconic words were not completely true. While the words were revolutionary for their time, by the word "men," they meant only white men. Excluded from the pursuit of happiness were people of color, women, and Native Americans. As white landowners expanded their land and power across America, others were forced from their land, forced to work with less pay or as slaves, and denied a voice in the government.

Slavery

In America's earliest days, slave traders abducted people from Africa and brought them via ship to America to be sold as slaves. The first slaves arrived in America in 1619.[1] Slavery is the practice of keeping people as property and forcing them to

The original Declaration of Independence still exists today, kept at the National Archives in Washington, DC.

work without pay. It's estimated that 6 to 7 million slaves were brought to the United States. Slaves had no rights of any kind. They could not own land, vote, or travel freely. They could be separated from their families and sold to others. They were not allowed to go to school, nor were they allowed to read or write. If they refused to work or attempted to escape, they could be tortured or killed.

Though some people began to question slavery after the American Revolution, the practice remained until the American Civil War. Abolitionists, or people who disagreed with slavery, began to protest in the 1780s, and their movement gained traction in the early 1800s. They helped slaves escape to the North, which was a part of the United States where slavery was

During the civil rights movement, African Americans marched through cities, demanding equal rights when it came to voting, jobs, education, housing, and more.

WE MARCH FOR
JOBS FOR ALL
A DECENT PAY
NOW!
WE MARCH FOR
JOBS FOR ALL
NOW!
WE DEMAND
AN END
POLICE
BRUTALITY
NOW!
WE MARCH FOR
JOBS
FOR ALL

Citizens vs. People in the Constitution

The US Constitution begins with "We the People," and most of the amendments use this language as well. "People" refers to a human in the United States, while "citizen" refers to a person with legal American citizenship. The Constitution and the amendments refer to people, not to citizens; therefore, all people receive the basic rights from the Constitution. This language has allowed people throughout history, such as people of color and women, to argue that they are people and therefore should be given the same rights as their white male counterparts.

illegal. The government agreed this was a states' rights issue, meaning that each state could decide for itself whether it would keep slavery legal or not. Eventually, as economic and social factors drove the country to split, the North and the South waged war with each other. The North was victorious, and it decided to make slavery illegal in order to cripple the Southern states and deprive them of their workforce.

On January 1, 1863, Abraham Lincoln delivered the Emancipation Proclamation, saying, "slaves within any State, or designated part of a State … shall be then, thenceforward, and forever free."[2] In order to make the proclamation stronger, the Constitution was amended to make slavery illegal in every state, rather than being chosen by the states. In 1865, the Thirteenth Amendment was ratified, officially ending slavery.

Even stronger laws were needed, so in 1868 the Fourteenth Amendment granted rights to all people, and it made anyone born in America a citizen. This allowed all slaves' children to be full citizens. In 1870, the Fifteenth Amendment granted the right to vote to black men, though many states added their own restrictions, and it did not grant the right to vote to women. It wasn't until the Voting Rights Act of 1965 that the laws that made it hard to vote were finally repealed.[3]

Women

While women were a vital part of American society starting from the time of the Revolutionary War, they were expected to stay at home and care for their families. On average they were paid less than men for the same work, a problem that persists today.[4] They were expected to stay out of politics, and they were denied the right to vote or serve in the military. A woman's husband owned her property, and she had to have his permission to do anything with it, such as sell it. Some states granted more rights than others.

Women protested and fought to be given the rights of full citizens since the days of the American Civil War. Another word for the right to vote is suffrage, so the women who fought for voting rights called themselves suffragettes. They were finally granted the right to vote in 1920, but it took much longer to gain access to military service. Title VII of the Civil Rights Act of 1964 made it illegal for employers to discriminate in hiring in regard to a variety of characteristics, including sex. This allowed women to hold the same jobs as men. In 1972, Title IX of the Federal Education Amendments passed, requiring women to be treated the same as men in education and in extracurricular activities, such as school sports.[5] In 2013, the ban against women in most military combat positions was lifted.

RISE UP
WOMAN.
NO MUD, NO LOTUS
KEEP YOUR LAWS
OFF OUR
STOP
WOMENS

Peaceful marching remains part of American democracy today. Women marched on Washington, DC, in 2017, after the election of Donald Trump.

Though women have made tremendous gains in civil rights, some of their struggles, such as pay equality, continue today.

Native Americans

Native Americans belong to the tribes of people who lived in America prior to the arrival of Europeans. As immigrants arrived and expanded their hold on the land, Native Americans were forcibly removed from their land. They also endured many battles with the incoming colonists. As Manifest Destiny—the idea that the settlers were owed more land—took hold and the pioneers began to move west and claim land, Native Americans were forced out of their homes and had to resettle elsewhere. Despite deals that supposedly gave them land in exchange for what they had lost, they were eventually placed onto reservations and could not leave. In 1887, President Grover Cleveland signed the Dawes Act, which let the government take reservations that had previously belonged to entire tribes and divide them up among individual Native American landowners. This represented an effort to force tribe members to live more like European Americans, and it radically changed the lifestyle of many tribes.

Native Americans were not considered citizens until 1924, when the Indian Citizenship Act was passed.[6] They were finally free to travel as they wanted. This granted them the right to vote as well, though some states still refused to allow it. In addition, restrictions such as poll taxes and mandatory literacy tests prevented many of them from doing so. It took the Voting Rights Act of 1965, and several future legislations, for Native Americans to gain full voting rights.[7]

In 1968, the Indian Civil Rights Act granted Native Americans basic rights under the Bill of Rights, requiring them to observe similar laws to the Constitution and Bill of Rights on their reservations, though they differ on how their courts are run. Native Americans still struggle with the government in regard to land rights and voter ID laws, which can make it difficult for people who live on reservations to vote.

Gay and Transgender Rights

Most recently, gay and transgender people have asked for equal rights. For much of America's history, homosexual and transgender people were considered by the government to be mentally ill, and they were denied the right to work in the government, marry, or have family health benefits. Hate crimes were common. Due to hostility toward them, they often tried to hide their true identities in order to function in society. In

Since the 1960s, LGBT people have marched to ensure they have the rights that others enjoy.

1973, homosexuality was removed as a mental illness from the *Diagnostic and Statistical Manual of Mental Disorders II* and the first gay rights bills were enacted shortly thereafter. However, marriage rights weren't granted until the 2000s, and it was done slowly, by individual states, until June 26, 2015, when the Supreme Court ruled that states have no right to prevent same-sex marriage.[8] In 2009, the Matthew Shepard and James Byrd Jr. Hate Crimes Prevention Act expanded hate crime legislation to cover LGBT people. Currently, members of the lesbian, gay, bisexual, and transgender community, which also includes various other orientations such as asexual and pansexual (LGBT+), are covered by antidiscrimination laws and hate crime laws, but they can vary by state.

Today, LGBT+ rights continue to be challenged, and transgender people are currently fighting to use facilities such as the bathroom that corresponds to their gender identity rather than their sex. They also fight for their right to serve in the military. The states continue to vote for and against their rights, but the government has not passed many official laws about how transgender people are to be treated.

People of color, Native Americans, women, and LGBT+ people have fought long and hard for equality in the United States. They started with few to no rights, and through centuries of struggle, they worked to change the laws in their favor and gain the same rights as their white male counterparts. They had to fight for a voice in the government and for their rights to employment, education, and property. The fight isn't over. Though we have made great gains over time, many groups still struggle for full equality.

CHAPTER 2

Black Americans' Civil Rights

When John Lewis was born in 1940, he had few rights as a black person. He was forced to attend segregated schools, and he could not use the same facilities as white students.[1] Though constitutional amendments had freed black people from slavery, newly implemented Jim Crow laws still denied them full rights. When Lewis marched in Selma, Alabama, as part of the civil rights movement, he could not have known what a pivotal role his actions would take in changing the laws and just how far he would go.

The Amendments

Before the Civil War, black people were forcibly taken from their homes and brought to the United States as slaves. In 1863, Lincoln's Emancipation Proclamation made the practice of slavery illegal, but the Southern states still resisted, writing their own state constitutions. Knowing a national law was needed, the Thirteenth Amendment was enacted in 1865. In order to be represented in the government, the Confederate states had to ratify it. The amendment officially ended slavery in the United States.

John Lewis marched for civil rights in the 1960s, and today he serves as a member of Congress, continuing to fight for equal rights and representation. He is shown here with the mug shots that were taken of him when he was arrested for participating in protests in the 1960s.

The Confederate states continued to try to deny rights to the newly freed slaves, and in order to enforce the laws, the federal government needed to strengthen the citizenship laws. In 1868, the Fourteenth Amendment was enacted, granting citizenship to every person born on American soil. It also granted all citizens "equal protection under the laws," which means that all people were protected by the Bill of Rights. Furthermore, it strengthened Congress's power to enforce the law, and it became the basis for future civil rights laws.

The Fifteenth Amendment, which was enacted in 1870, granted the right to vote to men of all races, though not to women. However, the language of the amendment was vague, and it allowed the states to devise their own voter requirements, which allowed for discrimination.[2] Many other laws needed to be passed to reach equality.

Civil Rights Acts of the 1800s

The end of the American Civil War and the Reconstruction Era that followed gave new rights to black people but also gave rise to the Ku Klux Klan, a white supremacist group. They, among others, used fear and violence to dissuade people of color from participating in society. In response, the government passed a series of civil rights acts that came to be known as the Force Acts or Ku Klux Klan Acts.

The first, the Civil Rights Act of 1870, prohibited discrimination in voter registration, allowing people to register

The 1870s saw the first civil rights laws for black men, allowing them to vote, but it would be nearly another hundred years before more such laws were passed.

to vote. The second, in 1871, placed all elections under the federal government's control, and it allowed marshals to keep order if things became violent at the polls.[3] The third, also in 1871, strengthened the Fourteenth Amendment by guaranteeing constitutional rights to all people and allowing the president to deploy the military or any means necessary to keep order.[4]

The Civil Rights Act of 1875 prohibited discrimination in public accommodations and allowed black people to vote; however, this law wasn't enforced and didn't help much. It was the last civil rights act to be passed for nearly 100 years.

Marching for Equality: The Civil Rights Movement of the 1960s

Following Reconstruction, the Southern states used the vague wording of the laws to create a system of "separate but equal" and overturn the Civil Rights Act of 1875. This allowed them to require separate facilities for black and white people. They could not use the same schools, restaurants, pools, drinking fountains, or train and streetcars. States could create their own rules for public transportation, such as requiring black people to sit at the back of the bus and give up their seats to white people. These were called Jim Crow laws after a racist theater character of the same name. "Jim Crow" eventually came to mean a racist concept of what all black Americans were like.

The law about train cars was challenged by the case *Plessy v. Ferguson* in the 1890s. In 1892, a black man named Homer Plessy bought a first-class ticket and attempted to board the train on the first-class car. When asked why he was doing so, he responded that he was an American citizen and should be allowed to sit in a first-class car. He was removed and arrested. He argued and lost his case before the Supreme Court in 1896; the court ruled that the idea of "separate but equal" was constitutional and that the discrimination was legal.[5]

"Separate but equal" remained the law of the land until the 1950s, when the Brown family challenged the Topeka Board of Education. They claimed that "separate but equal" was unequal because the white school nearest them wasn't equal at all—it was much better than the distant black school. In 1954, the Supreme Court agreed, and black people were allowed into white public schools for the first time.

In 1955, Rosa Parks was arrested in Montgomery, Alabama, for refusing to give up her bus seat to a white man. In response, black people boycotted, or refused to ride, Montgomery buses, causing the city financial hardship. This movement sparked more marches and protests, and despite violence aimed at Martin Luther King Jr. and other protesters, they persisted. The buses were desegregated in 1956—a victory that strengthened the civil rights movement.[6] To show that it was taking the movement seriously, Congress passing the Civil Rights Act of 1957. This act created the Commission on Civil Rights and the Civil Rights Division in the US Department of Justice, which allowed the government to investigate and address voting rights violations in the South.

As the 1960s began, so did sit-ins, a nonviolent form of protest. Black people sat at lunch counters and other whites-only places, refusing to move. One of the major organizers of the protests was the Student Nonviolent Coordinating Committee (SNCC), created at Shaw University in 1960. It was a group of student civil rights activists who focused on nonviolent protests, such as marches and sit-ins. They drew inspiration from the Indian activist Mahatma Gandhi, believing a nonviolent movement would bring their cause attention while minimizing the risk of people getting physically hurt. Protesters were subjected to violence, arrests, and counterprotests, but they persisted. The government began to integrate transportation,

Rosa Parks was arrested in 1955 for refusing to give up her seat on the bus to a white man.

schools, and universities, though it met resistance from much of the white populace.

Next, activists focused on voting rights. Though black people were registering to vote, they were hindered by violence from the Ku Klux Klan; literacy tests, which were difficult to pass with the weaker black education access; and poll taxes, which many could not afford.

In 1965, the Southern Christian Leadership Conference (SCLC) organized a series of marches from Selma, Alabama, to Montgomery, the state capital. In addition to demanding voting rights, the group was protesting the murder of unarmed protesters. The first march in Selma was led by John Lewis of SNCC and Reverend Hosea Williams of SCLC. It contained about 600 protesters.

As they marched, they were attacked by both the police and the surrounding crowds, resulting in many of them being beaten unconscious and leading to the day's later nickname, Bloody Sunday. The attack was televised, allowing people all over the country to see what the protesters were facing and causing support for the protesters to rise. Undaunted, they organized a second march, led by Dr. King and consisting of 2,500 marchers. They again were confronted by police, and the marchers turned around. Finally, the third march, which began with 8,000 people and ended with 25,000, ended with a successful arrival on the steps of the Alabama State Capitol Building.[7]

President Lyndon B. Johnson, inspired by the marches, ordered Congress to pass voting rights acts. Thus, in 1964, the Twenty-Fourth Amendment made all poll taxes illegal. In 1965, the Voting Rights Act outlawed literacy tests and other barriers to voting. Together, these measures allowed many more black people to register to vote. More marches followed to inspire black people to exercise that right. The Voting Rights Act was expanded in 1975 to include other races, such as Latinx, Asian,

Martin Luther King Jr. organized the March on Washington for Jobs and Freedom in 1963. The protest was instrumental in the passage of the Civil Rights Act the following year.

Civil Rights Act of 1968: The First Hate Crime Act

Passed as a memorial to Martin Luther King Jr. by President Johnson, the Civil Rights Act of 1968 made it a crime to threaten someone or use force to interfere with any person because of race, color, religion, or national origin, if the person is participating in a federally protected activity. This includes education, employment, jury service, or going to public places. It is considered the first hate crime law, because it was the first law to protect people if they were threatened in public. However, the act is far more commonly known for the part of it that's called the Fair Housing Act, which makes it illegal to discriminate against anyone trying to buy or rent a house based on their race, religion, national origin, or sex.[8]

and Native American people. It was expanded again in the Voting Rights Act of 2006, which requires bilingual election materials and education, to allow for greater voting rights for people who do not speak fluent English.[9] The full official title of the 2006 bill was the Fannie Lou Hamer, Rosa Parks, and Coretta Scott King Voting Rights Act Reauthorization and Amendments Act Of 2006 in honor of three important female civil rights leaders.

Although black Americans were slowly gaining rights, sometimes they had to fight hard for them—not just by protesting but also by taking certain issues to court when local governments violated their rights. For example, Mildred Jeter, a black woman, married Richard Loving, a white man, in the District of Columbia, which is not officially part of any state and has its own laws and regulations. When they returned to Virginia, they were sentenced to a year in jail because interracial marriage was illegal there, though they could avoid jail if they left Virginia. They took their case to the Supreme Court in 1967 in *Loving v. Virginia*, which ruled bans on interracial marriage unconstitutional.[10] The Court said that under the due process portion of Fourteenth Amendment, banning interracial marriage violated a citizen's rights. Chief Justice Earl Warren said, "The freedom to marry, or not marry, a person of another race resides with the individual, and cannot be infringed by the State."

People of color took extraordinary measures to gain equal rights and create the laws that protect them today. John Lewis, a congressman in Georgia and recipient of the Medal of Freedom, among other awards, looks back at his legacy of fighting for civil rights through his many books and speeches. He has said, "Every generation leaves behind a legacy. What that legacy will be is determined by the people of that generation. What legacy do you want to leave behind?"[11]

CHAPTER 3

Native Americans' Civil Rights

For centuries, America was an open land, and Native American tribes traveled freely across it. They had access to the land, resources, and freedom they needed. However, they started having skirmishes with European explorers from the late 1400s, as countries such as Spain, France, and England began to claim the land as their own.

Early Conflicts

Some of the Native Americans met settlers peacefully, while others were hostile. However, all Natives began to suffer loss of land and resources to the settlers. The French and the British fought over the land in the French and Indian War, which was part of the global Seven Years' War, drawing Native Americans into the conflict.

In 1785, the settlers signed the Treaty of Hopewell, which guaranteed the Cherokee their land and granted them protection; in 1791, the Cherokee gave up all the land outside of it in the Treaty of Holston.[1]

Conflict and colonization didn't stop. As the colonies grew bigger and America declared independence from Europe, people

Native American groups controlled the land—hunting, farming, and living on their own terms—until European colonists arrived and brought new laws with them.

living in the United States expanded their hold on the outlying land and forced the Native Americans inward. The white settlers believed in the idea of Manifest Destiny, the idea that they were destined to control all of America and that they alone had rights to settle and build on the land.

In 1814, Andrew Jackson and some Native Americans attacked the Creek tribe, who opposed the American expansion, driving them off their land and causing them to lose 20 million acres (8 million hecatres).[2] Later, as president, Jackson signed the Indian Removal Act in 1830, which gave plots of land to the Native Americans on the west side of the Mississippi River, in exchange for the land on the east side that they lost. Over the next decade, multiple tribes were forced off their land, often at gunpoint, and many died in the process.

Reservations

As the settlers expanded their hold, there wasn't enough land for the Native Americans to be moved to. In 1851, the Indian Appropriations Act was passed, creating reservations, or designated areas where the Native Americans were forced to live. They were not allowed to leave the reservations without permission.[3] Different tribes were forced into the same areas, causing friction. Native Americans were encouraged to speak English and farm rather than hunt. It was very difficult to hold on to their culture in this setting.

The Dawes Act in 1887 further hurt tribal culture by breaking reservations up into small plots for individual Native American families to own and farm. Much of the land was poor, however, and unsuitable for farming. What's more, in the process of breaking up the reservations, much of the land was sold to whites. By dismantling the reservations and trying to integrate Natives into white society, the Dawes Act effectively removed the tribes as legal entities and denied them a voice in the government.

In 1924, to thank Native Americans for serving in the US military during World War I, Congress authorized a survey to

Reservations were created in 1851 as more white settlements pushed Native Americans off of land that had always been theirs.

see what life on the reservations was like. This survey, which was called the Meriam Survey, found that living conditions were horrible for many people, due mainly to lack of funds and lack of power for the reservations' leaders to enact change. In response to the survey's findings, the Indian Reorganization Act was passed in 1934. It gave surplus land to the tribes and restored their ability to govern themselves and write their own laws and constitutions within their boundaries. It also gave government financial aid for infrastructure within the reservations. This system continues today, though living conditions on the reservations are generally still not as good as they are elsewhere in the country.

Citizenship

Despite being the original people on the land, it was a long time before Native Americans were granted American citizenship. Since they were considered a separate entity from the American people and isolated on the reservations, they were denied the right to vote and the rights of American citizens. The Fifteenth Amendment in 1870 granted citizens of all races the right to vote, but Native Americans were not considered citizens.[4]

Citizenship was not granted until 1924, under the Snyder Act, also known as the Indian Citizenship Act. This act allowed Native Americans to leave reservations whenever they wanted. Even then, they weren't fully granted the rights of citizens. Individual states decided whether or not Native Americans could vote at all. Each state took decades to decide. In fact, the last state to allow Native Americans to vote was New Mexico in 1962.[5]

Even when New Mexico agreed to let them vote, Native Americans faced the same issues African Americans did, such as literacy tests and poll taxes, which kept them from voting.

Native Americans, like other groups that faced discrimination, have always fought for their rights. Here, Osage men meet with President Calvin Coolidge in 1925.

In 1968, the Indian Civil Rights Act declared that Native Americans had the same rights other citizens did under the Bill of Rights. It says that a tribe may not make laws that remove civil rights from people living on reservations. This allows them freedom of speech and religion, the right to a jury trial, freedom of search and seizure, and protection from cruel and unusual punishment. However, there are a few differences from the Bill of Rights. A tribe may establish a religion, rather than maintaining a separation between church and state. A person

The Voting Rights Act of 1965

Even though Native Americans were allowed to vote in all states, poll taxes and literacy tests made it very difficult for people in poverty, black people, and Native Americans to vote prior to 1965, when President Johnson signed the Voting Rights Act. The new law ended literacy tests and created other protections for voters. Poll taxes were separately outlawed by the Twenty-Fourth Amendment and a 1966 court decision. These measures allowed Americans to vote in greater numbers. The Voting Rights Act was strengthened again in the 1970s and 1980s.[6]

accused of a crime may pay for their own lawyer, but the tribe does not have to provide one, and civil cases do not have to be held before a jury.[7] This law is considered controversial because it gives the federal government the right to intervene in tribal affairs, which some Native Americans resent.

The Indian Self-Determination and Education Assistance Act followed in 1975, which allowed Native American tribal governments to negotiate with the federal government and create their own schools.[8] In 1978, the Religious Freedom Act allowed them to establish their own religions and to designate sacred sites, an act that was strengthened in 1993. The Indian Child Welfare Act was also created in 1978, and it allows tribes to decide if children can be removed from a family and who can adopt them, which helps keep tribal cultures and families intact.

The Civil Rights Movement

What brought about this change? Like other people of color, Native Americans became more active in forming civil rights

In 1969, Native Americans sailed to the island of Alcatraz in San Francisco Bay and occupied the former prison for nineteen months as a form of protest.

protest groups in the 1960s. The American Indian Movement was especially active. Its goals were to revitalize tribal cultures, gain economic independence, and take back land that had been taken unjustly.[9] They organized many high-profile protests.

Rather than just marching, the American Indian Movement was known for occupying locations. In 1969, ninety members of the group sailed out to Alcatraz Island in San Francisco Bay, and occupied the area for nineteen months. They argued that by white people's standards, the island was ideal for a reservation, as it lacked resources such as transportation, water, sanitation, education, jobs, and the ability to be farmed, and it was too small for the population. This comparison was used to draw attention to the poor living conditions on the government-created reservations.[10] The group demanded that the land be given over to Natives and that government funds be given to create a Native American cultural center and school. The protesters organized a society and stayed until eventually federal marshals removed them, but the protest drew a great amount of attention to their cause, and it set the stage for other such protests.[11]

In 1970, the protesters occupied Mount Rushmore, wanting to reclaim the land for the Sioux tribe, to which it had originally been promised in the 1868 Treaty of Fort Laramie. They also occupied Plymouth Rock in a protest known as the National Day of Mourning. This was the result of the Commonwealth of Massachusetts censoring a speech to be given by a Wampanoag man named Frank James at a celebration of the Pilgrims' landing. The officials felt his speech wouldn't be celebratory enough. This protest is repeated yearly at Plymouth Rock as a reminder of the resources, land, and culture that was taken from the Native Americans.[12]

In 1972, the Trail of Broken Treaties Caravan, a combination of various Native American civil rights groups, held a six-day protest and occupation of the Bureau of Indian Affairs in Washington. It was followed in 1973 by the occupation of Wounded Knee, South Dakota—the site of the 1890 Wounded Knee Massacre. It lasted seventy-one days, and like the Alcatraz occupation, it was meant to draw attention to the terrible living conditions and poor economic opportunities of Native Americans on reservations and the broken promises of the government.[13] It was considered one of the most successful protests.

In 1978, a few thousand marchers walked from San Francisco to Washington, DC, in the Longest Walk. By the time they reached DC, there were 30,000 people marching. They were protesting proposed laws that would strip away some of their tribal government, restrict their hunting and fishing rights, and close their hospitals and schools, as well as drawing attention to the overall cause.[14] Celebrities and politicians joined in, and the protests continued peacefully for two weeks. In the end, none of the bills were passed.

Native Americans have often been used as symbols and mascots for sports teams. In 1991, the National Coalition on Racism in Sports and Media was formed to combat this, and many high school, college, and state teams have removed these mascots or changed their names in the following decades, though some still resist.

Though progress has been made, many Native Americans are still relegated to reservations, and those reservations are often threatened by groups who wish to build there or drill for oil. For example, in 2016, Natives and non-Natives joined forces to occupy Standing Rock, North Dakota, where an oil pipeline was going to be built. President Barack Obama denied a permit that would allow the pipeline to be built, but when President Donald Trump took office, he reversed that decision. Not long after the pipeline was built, it ruptured, spilling oil into the surrounding soil and water—just as activists feared it would.

CHAPTER 4

Women's Civil Rights

In 1848, the Seneca Falls Convention reinterpreted the Declaration of Independence. Their own Declaration of Sentiments declared, "We hold these truths to be self-evident, that all men *and women* are created equal, that they are endowed by their creator with certain inalienable rights, that among these are life, liberty, and the pursuit of happiness." It listed grievances against men, declaring that they took rights, property, and voice away from women, and it demanded fair representation in government for women.[1]

The convention was a mix of women and men led by Elizabeth Cady Stanton and Lucretia Mott, two strong suffrage leaders. Following the American Civil War, women, who had long been denied a voice in the country they helped to build, saw that the amendments were shifting power to all men, and they knew their time had come to fight. It would be a long and hard journey.

Women's Suffrage

The Civil War came to a close, and the Fourteenth and Fifteenth Amendments declared that all men were citizens and that

In 1848, the Seneca Falls Convention gathered women together. They were determined to have equal rights.

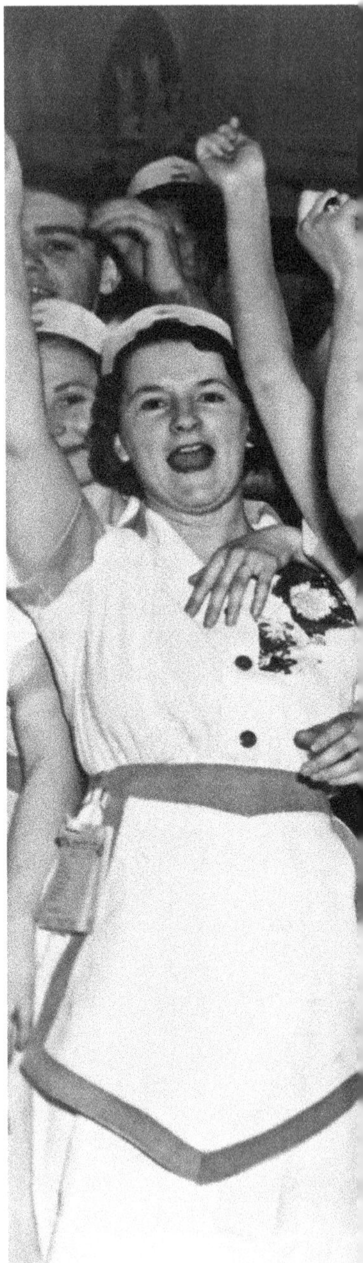

black men could now vote. Many women took issue with the amendments, declaring that if all men were now equal, women, who also worked hard to make society run in America, should have the same voice. Susan B. Anthony and Elizabeth Cady Stanton worked hard to rally women into a cohesive group in 1869.[2] Although these women were influential, they have been criticized for not being more inclusive of women of color, as their movement generally prioritized white women.

In 1890, the National American Woman Suffrage Association (NAWSA) was formed, led by Elizabeth Cady Stanton. Over the following decades, NAWSA worked tirelessly to win women the right to vote. The territory of Wyoming had already given voting rights to women in 1869. In the 1890s, Colorado, Utah, and Idaho followed.[3] These early successes were limited to the West because it was argued that the pioneer lifestyle there required women to work with the men, so they should have the right to vote. However, other states, especially in the South, resisted. Groups formed all over, marching and protesting. One group, the National Women's Party, used stronger methods, such as picketing the White House and going on hunger strikes. One of the strongest arguments for women's suffrage came during World War I, when women worked alongside men to support the war effort. They used their work in the war to showcase that they,

Like men, women would often strike if they weren't happy with job conditions. In 1938, the Fair Labor Standards Act was passed.

too, were valuable members of society and that they deserved an equal voice.

At last, in 1920, the government passed the Nineteenth Amendment to the Constitution, which granted all women the right to vote. This was the first of many legal changes that would grant women greater freedom.

Working Women

In the early days of America, women were largely left to work in the home, and they were forbidden from certain jobs, such as practicing law. They also were limited in the number of hours they could work outside the home. In 1932, the National Recovery Act forbade more than one family member from having a government job, which resulted in many women losing their jobs. Though women both needed and wanted to work, they were often denied the opportunity.

In 1938, the Fair Labor Standards Act guaranteed a minimum wage regardless of sex. This helped with blue collar jobs, but it took until 1963 for pay to be equal in most jobs.[4] That year, the Equal Pay Act was passed, promising equal wages for the same work, regardless of race, color, religion, national origin, or sex. In 1964, Title VII of the Civil Rights Act passed, forbidding job discrimination on the basis of race, color, religion, national origin, or sex. In 1965, Executive Order 11246 extended these protections to government jobs. These two acts allowed women to work in a much larger array of jobs, though the acts were not always enforced the way they were written.

Employers could fire women if they were pregnant until 1978, when the Pregnancy Discrimination Act banned the practice. In 1993, the Family and Medical Leave Act allowed people to take unpaid time off from a job to take care of a sick family member, recover from illness, or have a baby. In 2015, it was expanded to cover same-sex families.[5] This was a tremendous boost to women's rights because it allowed women to have children without risking their jobs.

Women served in the military as nurses and support from the time of the American Revolution, but it wasn't until 1948, under the Women's Armed Services Integration Act, that women could serve in the military full time. The act limited the number of women who could serve, however, and it prevented women from taking on combat roles. The combat restrictions were lifted for air and sea missions in the early 1990s, but they were reaffirmed for ground missions in 1994. In practice, however, women in noncombat roles would often find themselves in combat situations. Acknowledging this reality and the unfairness of its combat restrictions, the Department of Defense began opening more combat roles to women in 2013. This process culminated in 2016, when all combat roles were

The Equal Credit Opportunity Act of 1974

Imagine you're a woman with her own job, earning money for your household. You go to the bank to open a checking account or get a credit card. The employee demands to know if you're married, and then says you can't open one without your husband's signature. If you are single, divorced, or widowed, they demand you bring a man to cosign. Before 1974, a woman couldn't open a bank account on her own! In 1974, the Equal Credit Opportunity Act passed, which makes it illegal to discriminate based on a person's gender, race, or origin. Finally, women and people of color could have their own bank accounts. However, it's not perfect; a 2012 study says women still pay more interest on credit cards than men.[6]

Margaret Sanger opened the first US birth control clinic for women in 1916. She believed women should have a right to choose if and when to have children.

opened to women, with no exceptions. Whether or not women can be drafted is still under debate.[7]

Women's Family and Heath Rights

For most of America's history, women's health was largely overlooked, and women were left to their own devices for menstrual and birth care as well as overall health. Birth control was illegal until 1965 for married women and until 1972 for single women, but women often used dangerous or illegal methods before then.[8]

The first American birth control clinic was opened in 1916 by Margaret Sanger. She argued that poverty and high birth rates risked women's lives, and they should be able to choose when to have children or even whether they wanted to have them at all. She also founded the American Birth Control League in 1921, which would later become Planned Parenthood. Birth control pills were invented in 1960, giving women much greater control over their own reproductive choices. In 1973, *Roe v. Wade* was decided, allowing women access to legal abortion. In 2010, the Affordable Care Act mandated that health insurance provide free birth control. The ability to use safe birth control allowed women to have safer pregnancies and childbirth and work as they chose.[9]

Women are still often subjected to violence, either in domestic situations or as gender-related hate crimes. In 1994, the Violence Against Women Act was passed, which set aside funding for women's shelters, rape prevention programs, and programs to educate people about domestic violence. It was renewed and expanded in 2013 to cover Native Americans, same-sex couples, and victims of human trafficking. However, it lapsed in 2018 under the Trump administration.

Women's Education

Schools today are open to women and men taking any classes that please them, but it wasn't always so. Starting in the 1800s, women could attend school through college, but in practice, many schools found ways to exclude women. High schools often segregated students into "gender-appropriate classes," such as home economics for girls and industrial arts for boys, and women's career choices after school were limited.

As the civil rights movement pushed for more rights for women, girls began to insist on having equal access to classes. In 1972, the government enacted Title IX of the Federal Education Amendments. Title IX protects people from discrimination

Forty years after the passage of Title IX, Hillary Clinton, shown here, and others came together to celebrate its continuing impact on the country.

based on sex in education programs or activities that receive federal financial assistance. This means that any school that takes government money must grant equal opportunities to men and women. Title IX helped open many new career fields to women.

Teachers needed retraining, too, as their biases sometimes led them to discourage girls from engaging in math and science. Seeing that the education system needed reform, in 1994 Congress adopted the Gender Equity in Education Act, which was used to retrain teachers about gender bias, create science and math programs for girls, and train teachers and students in preventing sexual harassment at school.[10]

Women were often overlooked in school sports as well. In 1997, Title IX was expanded to cover school sports. It states that in order to receive funding, athletic programs must include a roughly equal number of opportunities for male and female participants.

These laws allow women greater freedom in their careers, their families, and their education. They allow women to have greater freedom in making money and taking care of themselves. They can participate in the government, which allows them greater flexibility in helping create laws to protect themselves. However, the laws are not consistently enforced, which means that women still struggle to make the same money or have the same independence that men do. While rights for women have come a long way, there is still work to be done.

Chapter 5

Gay and Transgender Rights

One evening in October 1998, a young gay man named Matthew Shepard walked into a bar in Laramie, Wyoming. He was meeting some other LGBT+ students from the University of Wyoming to plan an LGBT Awareness Week. When they left, he started chatting with Russell Henderson and Aaron McKinney, who pretended to be gay. They lured him outside and into their car, where they took him to a remote area, tied him to a fence, and beat him to death. Evidence presented in the trial showed they were homophobic and they murdered him for his sexual orientation.[1] His brutal death shocked the country and drew attention to the violence and discrimination LGBT+ Americans were facing.

The Stonewall Inn

Before 1973, homosexuality was classified as a mental illness, so the rights of LGBT+ people were largely ignored, and "homosexual activity" in public was illegal in many places. In fact, people could be arrested in New York for not wearing

In 1998, the murder of Matthew Shepard drew the nation's attention to the LGBT+ fight for equal rights.

"gender-appropriate" clothing. In the 1950s, gay rights groups such as the Mattachine Society and the Daughters of Bilitis were formed, but LGBT+ rights continued to be ignored, and many LGBT+ people hid their sexual orientation, fearing arrest and violence.[2]

Many LGBT+ people sought out gay bars as places to express themselves freely and avoid the police. The bars were frequently raided by the police and shut down for "disorderly behavior" or for not having a liquor license, partially because many of these bars were owned by the mafia.[3] One famous gay bar was the Stonewall Inn in New York City.

The Stonewall Inn was a large bar that welcomed transgender people as well as gay people, which was rare at the time. On June 28, 1969, the police raided the Stonewall Inn, citing a lack of a liquor license. Finding people violating the "gender-appropriate clothing" rule, the police began arresting them. Many people who frequented the area were tired of police interference and began to surround the bar. When a police officer struck a woman he was arresting, the crowd rioted. People barricaded themselves inside the bar while the riot raged outside. Eventually they were rescued, but thousands of people returned for several days to protest. These protests drew national attention to LGBT+ rights, and multiple LGBT+ rights groups formed that still exist today, such as the Human Rights Campaign, GLAAD (originally Gay and Lesbian Alliance Against Defamation),

In 1969, the Stonewall Inn was raided by police, who arrested LGBT+ people for violating gender dress codes. Riots and protests followed.

and PFLAG (Parents, Families and Friends of Lesbians and Gays).

Harvey Milk

In 1977, Harvey Milk was elected to the San Francisco Board of Supervisors. He was one of the first openly gay men elected into the government. For the first time, LGBT+ people had representation, and more attention was drawn to their cause. Prior to being elected, when gay people were unable to open businesses, Milk organized fairs to promote LGBT+ businesses. He was well-known in the community.

During Milk's political career, a California senator named John Briggs presented Proposition 6, which would have mandated firing gay teachers. Milk organized protests, and as he did so, his movement grew in popularity. The proposition was defeated.

An eloquent speaker, Milk was able to bring together groups of people of color, women, and LGBT+ people to campaign for work equality and for unions to hire more gay employees. He became a voice for equality.

Throughout his career, Milk received death threats, and in 1978, Dan White, a former city supervisor, assassinated Milk because White blamed him for the loss of his job. His death spurred a multitude of gay rights marches.[4] The first National March on Washington for Gay Rights was in 1979. In 1982, Wisconsin became the first state to ban discrimination based on sexual orientation.

Military Service

In 1993, President Bill Clinton signed a policy known as "Don't Ask, Don't Tell." The policy was intended to lift a ban against gay people serving in the military. However, it said that gay people could now only serve if they kept their sexuality a secret.

Thus, openly gay soldiers still couldn't serve in the military until 2011, when Don't Ask, Don't Tell was overturned. Transgender people, however, were not included in this change.

Hate Crime Laws

The Civil Rights Act of 1968 was considered to be the first hate crime act, a law that specifically protected people from

LGBT+ people have made good strides toward equality, but transgender people have often been left out. Like others before them, they have marched to fight for their freedoms.

crimes directed at them for the color of their skin. This law was strengthened by the Hate Crimes Sentencing Enhancement Act of 1993, which allowed courts to impose harsher sentences on people convicted of hate crimes.[5]

The strongest hate crimes act was the Matthew Shepard and James Byrd Jr. Hate Crimes Prevention Act of 2009. Its name commemorates the death of Matthew Shepard in Wyoming and the brutal death of James Byrd Jr., a man who was dragged to death behind a pickup truck by white men because he was black. This act expanded the hate crimes act to include race, religion, gender, sexual orientation or identity, and disability. It was the first to allow federal prosecution of these crimes.[6]

Gay Marriage

Gay people have fought hard for their rights to marriage, including shared health benefits and the ability to visit a spouse in the hospital. In September 1996, President Clinton signed the Defense of Marriage Act (DOMA), which defined marriage as a union of one man and one woman and denied federal benefits to same-sex couples. However, not all states agreed with the policy, and they began to enact their own laws. In December of the same year, Hawaii became the first state to recognize that gay couples should have the same rights as heterosexual couples. This began a battle across the country as states argued among themselves about whether or not gay couples could marry. Though there was a national precedent, it became a states' rights issue.

It took until the 2000s for gay marriage to be legalized. Virginia recognized civil unions in 2000, which allowed for marital benefits without being called "marriage," and Massachusetts allowed the first gay marriage in 2004. In the following decade, some states legalized gay marriage while others reinforced the ban on it. In June of 2015, the Supreme

In 2015, when the Supreme Court ruled that states cannot ban gay marriage, the White House was lit up in rainbow colors to celebrate.

Court ruled that states cannot ban gay marriage.[7] This effectively legalized gay marriage across the United States.

Transgender Rights

Though gay, lesbian, bisexual, and people of other orientations have made great gains in their civil rights, transgender people have often been left out. Transgender people identify with a gender that does not match their biological sex. For example, a doctor may say a baby is male at birth, but that person may grow up identifying as a woman and not a man.

Gender Identity vs. Sexual Orientation in the Law

Sexual orientation and gender identity are treated differently under the law. Some rights that are equal are the right to marry, protection under hate crimes laws, and, since the passage of the Affordable Care Act, health insurance. However, some states still deny some forms of health care to transgender people, and gender reassignment care may not be covered. Gay and bisexual people can currently serve in the military, but transgender people have been alternately banned from serving and reinstated multiple times over the course of the Trump administration. In many places, transgender people fight for their right to use the bathroom that aligns with their identity. Many states have antidiscrimination laws, but not all of them do, and enforcement isn't always consistent.[8]

States differ as to the rights that transgender people have. Many have antidiscrimination laws, though their protections vary by state. For example, in Maine, transgender discrimination is banned in housing, education, credit, employment, and access to public places, but Nevada does not protect credit or education.[9] Transgender people can also be excluded from areas of health care.

One of the major arguments among the states is the "bathroom wars," an argument about whether transgender people should use the bathroom of the gender they identify with or of their sex. In 2016, a North Carolina court ruled that transgender students could not use the bathroom of their gender identity. The Department of Justice (DOJ) ruled that banning students from their chosen bathroom violates Title IX, which protects people from sex discrimination in schools. For that reason, the DOJ required all schools to allow transgender students to use the bathroom of their identity. In 2017, President Donald Trump reversed the decision, implying that Title IX does not apply to transgender students.[10] The decision is now left up to the individual states as of 2019.

At the national level, in 2016, the Pentagon said that transgender people could openly serve in the military. However, in 2017, President Trump declared a ban on transgender people serving. Courts filed injunctions to allow transgender people to enter the military while the cases were being heard. In January 2019, the Supreme Court allowed the ban to proceed, and in April of the same year, the policy became official. As of April 12, 2019, recruits who identify as transgender must serve as their biological sex, not their preferred gender, and they will be rejected if they have already transitioned. Active service members who had already started transitioning before that date were allowed to continue transitioning and serving, though.[11]

It's important to note that gay and transgender people, while often placed in the same group, are treated differently under the law. The fight continues for their equal rights.

Chapter 6

Where Are We Today?

Civil rights laws throughout history are the result of extraordinary people making extraordinary choices. They marched, protested, endured violence and backlash from society, and fought tirelessly to make their lives and the lives of those around them equal. We celebrate their accomplishments and look back at their progress, but we're not fully equal yet.

People of Color and Women

People of color and women still face violence and pay inequality. While laws say that they're equal with the rest of society, they are often inconsistently enforced or ignored. Sometimes discrimination shows itself in new ways.

New civil rights groups continue to form. One of the most prominent groups as of 2019 is Black Lives Matter, a group that works to promote awareness of the discrimination and violence black people still face. Like groups before them, they organize marches and protests, and they focus on addressing racial violence, especially from police. The group formed 2013 in response to unarmed black people being killed by police officers. Cases such as those of Tamir Rice, Sandra Bland, and Michael Brown have mobilized their protests.[1]

Today, the Human Rights Campaign is the largest LGBT+ civil rights group in the United States.

Studies find that black, Latinx, and Native American people are statistically much more likely to be killed by police than white people. In a study published by the *Journal of Epidemiology & Community Health*, researchers found that Native American people were killed by police at the highest rate in the country—7.8 per million. Black people were second at 7.2 per million. Compare this to the rate of 2.9 per million killed by police in the white population.[2] Protests continue in the hopes of drawing attention to and ending this violence.

People of color also face a gap in pay equality. In 2015, studies found that black men earned only 73 percent of what white men do, and Latinx men earn 69 percent. Men of all races continue to earn more than all women; Latinx women earned the least of any group.[3]

Currently, the pay gap for white women is 80 percent on average, meaning women earn 80 cents to every man's dollar for the same work. Black women earn 61 percent, Native American women earn 58 percent, and Hispanic women earn 53 percent. Discrepancies were found across every profession, and they vary by state. In 2017, California had the smallest gap at 89 percent; Louisiana had the largest at

White women continue to make less income than white men, and black women and Latina women remain even further behind.

69 percent.[4] Though the Equal Pay Act promised equal wages, it is frequently not enforced. Employers often use prior work history and education to set wages, which is one factor in the gap. This has been challenged in court; in *Dukes v. Walmart* in 2011, 1.5 million women sued Walmart for discriminatory wages. The Supreme Court ruled that even though the women may have been paid less, they couldn't rule that the entire company was discriminatory. Many of the people are filing individual lawsuits in an attempt to recover wages.[5]

Though many groups fight these policies, in an uncertain economy, many women and people of color fear losing their jobs if they fight for equal wages.

Native Americans, Land Rights, and Voting

In addition to fighting against a pay gap, Native Americans fight for the rights to their land. Two of the most recent battles have been over the Keystone XL Pipeline and Bears Ears National Monument in Utah.

The Keystone XL is an aboveground oil pipeline meant to bring oil from Canada to Texas. Supporters of the pipeline claim it will bring a great amount of oil into America, creating jobs. In addition to environmental concerns, some of the pipeline crosses through Native American lands, and they have not agreed to its construction. The Fort Belknap Indian Community of Montana and the Rosebud Sioux Tribe of South Dakota argue that since the land belongs to their tribe and they own the water rights, the government has no right to build the pipeline there. They also say they do not agree to the environmental risks associated with an oil pipeline.[6] As of 2019, this issue is still being fought in court, and the pipeline has not yet been built.

The Bears Ears National Monument in Utah was declared a National Monument by President Barack Obama in 2016. It contains a variety of Native American historical sites.

In 2017, President Trump announced a plan to reduce the monument's size by 85 percent, or more than 1 million acres (404,700 hectares).[7] While some sites would remain protected, many others would be left exposed. Trump argued that the federal government went too far in protecting so much land and that it should be available for drilling and development. The Hopi, Navajo Nation, Ute Mountain Ute Tribe, Pueblo of Zuni, and the Ute Indian Tribe took steps to sue, claiming that the land is sacred to the Native Americans and rightly belongs to them.[8] Many lawsuits were still pending as of 2019.

In addition to land rights, Native Americans continue to face voting discrimination. In North Dakota, a law is in place that requires people to show an ID with a valid street address to vote. Many Native Americans on reservations use PO boxes rather than a standard address, and this, mixed with a long travel distance to voting sites and high poverty, keeps them

The Transgender Military Ban

Even after the "Don't Ask, Don't Tell" policy was repealed, transgender soldiers still weren't allowed to serve openly in the military. That changed in 2016, when the Obama administration announced a reversal of that ban. However, President Trump reinstated the ban on transgender soldiers in 2017, saying they "erode military cohesion."[9] In January 2019, the Supreme Court upheld the ban and disqualified transgender people from military service. The fight now lies in the House and Senate, which continue to bring bills forward to reverse the ban. What do you think? Should all people be allowed to serve their country?

In 2017, President Trump announced a plan to rescind the right of transgender people to serve in the US military. This was met with court fights and protests.

from voting.[10] This is true in other states as well. The Native American Voting Rights Act was presented in 2018 to allow tribal IDs to be used and grant easier access to voting sites. The bill was not voted on that year and was reintroduced in 2019.

LGBT+ Rights

Under President Trump, the federal government has attempted to rescind some LGBT protections, but individual states continue to adjust their laws to enhance the rights of LGBT+ people. Some states, such as Kansas, have banned discrimination in the workplace. Others have enacted laws to make it easier for same-sex couples to obtain embryos to have children.[11]

Many states have banned or are in the process of banning conversion therapy, a practice of trying to change someone's sexual orientation from homosexual or bisexual to heterosexual using psychological or religious means. Overall, psychiatrists and doctors have found the practice to be ineffective.[12] Worse, it has actually proven to be dangerous; conversion therapy is known to increase depression and suicidal tendencies in the people it is used on. Many states are banning the practice completely in order to protect LGBT+ people.

The transgender community continues to fight for their rights to keep their jobs and for future transgender people to get jobs. In addition, transgender people fight for the right to

If history has taught us anything, it's that people will not be silenced. They fight for what's important. What will you fight for?

use the bathroom of their identity. This right varies by state. Transgender students continue to struggle with discrimination in schools and on sports teams. Some health insurance plans exclude treatments for transgender people, especially for gender reassignment procedures. Though many states have created laws to help protect transgender people, they are often inconsistently enforced or change from state to state. LGBT+ rights remain largely a states' rights issue.

What Can We Do?

America has come a long way in terms of civil rights. Many laws affect how people vote, where they can go, their education, how they get jobs, how much they are paid, and how they are protected from violence and prejudice. People of color, women, Native Americans, and LGBT+ people have all fought for and gained tremendous freedom over the past centuries. Though these laws have helped bring gains, we still have progress to make to ensure that everyone in America is equal.

Think about the people in your life who still struggle. Will there be protests in the future? Will pay and voting inequalities be eliminated? What can you do for yourself and for the people who still fight?

CHRONOLOGY

1848 At the Seneca Falls Convention, a gathering of reformers call for equal rights for women.

1851 The Indian Appropriations Act creates reservations for Native Americans.

1865 The Thirteenth Amendment is ratified, officially ending slavery.

1868 The Fourteenth Amendment gives citizenship to all people born on American soil and grants them equal rights under the Constitution.

1869 The territory of Wyoming becomes the first place in the United States to give women the right to vote.

1870 The Fifteenth Amendment grants all men the right to vote.

1896 *Plessy v. Ferguson* solidifies segregation and the idea of "separate but equal."

1920 The Nineteenth Amendment grants women the right to vote and full citizenship rights.

1924 The Indian Citizenship Act (Snyder Act) grants citizenship to Native Americans.

1934 The Indian Reorganization Act gives reservations the right to govern themselves and gives them government aid.

1938 The Fair Labor Standards Act gives a minimum wage regardless of sex.

1954 *Brown v. Board of Education of Topeka* outlaws the racial segregation of schools.

1963 The Equal Pay Act is passed, promising equal wages for the same work, regardless of race, color, religion, national origin, or sex.

1964 Title VII of the Civil Rights Act forbids employment discrimination regardless of race, color, religion, national origin, or sex.

1965 The Voting Rights Act makes literacy tests illegal and creates other measures protecting voting rights.

1967 *Loving v. Virginia* goes to the Supreme Court, and the court rules that interracial marriage is legal under the Fourteenth Amendment.

1968 The Indian Civil Rights Act grants Native Americans the same basic rights as other citizens.

1968 The Civil Rights Act of 1968, also known as the Fair Housing Act, forbids people selling or renting real estate from discriminating against people of color.

1969 A police raid of the Stonewall Inn in New York City sparks intense protests for LGBT+ rights.

1972 Title IX of the Federal Education Amendments is enacted, which forbids discrimination in schools that receive federal funding.

1973 *Roe v. Wade* gives women access to legal abortion.

1975 The Indian Self-Determination and Education Assistance Act allows Native American tribal governments to negotiate with the federal government and create their own schools.

1978 The Religious Freedom Act allows Native Americans to establish their own religion and to designate sacred sites.

1978 The Indian Child Welfare Act allows tribes to decide if children can be removed from a home and who can adopt them.

1994 The Violence Against Women Act sets aside funding for women's shelters, rape prevention programs, and programs to educate communities about domestic violence.

1994 The Gender Equity in Education Act is used to retrain teachers about gender bias, create science and math programs for girls, and train teachers and students in preventing sexual harassment at school.

1996 The Defense of Marriage Act (DOMA) states that marriage is between one man and one woman and denies federal benefits to same-sex couples.

2009 The Matthew Shepard and James Byrd Jr. Hate Crimes Prevention Act expands the federal definition of hate crimes.

2015 DOMA is overturned, allowing same-sex couples the same rights to marriage benefits as heterosexual couples.

2016 Women are permitted in all combat roles in the military.

2019 A ban on transgender military service that was announced in 2017 is upheld by the courts.

CHAPTER NOTES

CHAPTER 1: America's Early Days: Who Had Rights?

1. "Slavery in America," History.com, updated January 31, 2019, www.history.com/topics/black-history/slavery.
2. "Slavery in America," History.com.
3. "15th Amendment," History.com, last updated September 12, 2018, www.history.com/topics/black-history/fifteenth-amendment.
4. "Pay Equity and Discrimination," Institute of Women's Policy Research, 2019, iwpr.org/issue/employment-education-economic-change/pay-equity-discrimination.
5. Susan Milligan, "Stepping Through History: A Timeline of Women's Rights," *US News & World Report*, January 20, 2017, www.usnews.com/news/the-report/articles/2017-01-20/timeline-the-womens-rights-movement-in-the-us.
6. "Native American History Timeline," History.com, January 15, 2019, www.history.com/topics/native-american-history/native-american-timeline.
7. "Elections ... the American Way: Voting Rights for Native Americans," Library of Congress, accessed on March 2, 2019, www.loc.gov/teachers/classroommaterials/presentationsandactivities/presentations/elections/voting-rights-native-americans.html.
8. "LGBT Rights Milestones Fast Facts," CNN Library, updated February 18, 2019, www.cnn.com/2015/06/19/us/lgbt-rights-milestones-fast-facts/index.html.

CHAPTER 2: Black Americans' Civil Rights

1. "Biography," Congressman John Lewis, 2019, johnlewis.house.gov/john-lewis/biography.
2. "Landmark Legislation: Thirteenth, Fourteenth, & Fifteenth Amendments," United States Senate, 2019, www.senate.gov/artandhistory/history/common/generic/CivilWarAmendments.htm.

3. History, Art and Archives: United States House of Representatives, "Constitutional Amendments and Major Civil Rights Acts of Congress Referenced in Black Americans in Congress," The Office of the Historian, 2019, history.house.gov/Exhibitions-and-Publications/BAIC/Historical-Data/Constitutional-Amendments-and-Legislation.
4. History, Art and Archives: United States House of Representatives, "The Ku Klux Klan Act of 1871," the Office of the Historian, 2019, history.house.gov/HistoricalHighlight/Detail/15032451486?ret=True.
5. Melvin I. Urofsky, "Jim Crow Law," *Encyclopedia Britannica*, 2019, www.britannica.com/event/Jim-Crow-law.
6. Femi Lewis, "Civil Rights Movement Timeline from 1951 to 1959," *ThoughtCo*, June 14, 2018, www.thoughtco.com/civil-rights-movement-timeline-1951-to-1959-45418.
7. "Marching for the Vote," United States Civil Rights Trail, accessed on August 9, 2019, civilrightstrail.com/experience/marching-for-the-right-to-vote.
8. "Hate Crime Laws," United States Department of Justice, October 15, 2018, www.justice.gov/crt/hate-crime-laws.
9. History, Art and Archives: United States House of Representatives, "Constitutional Amendments and Major Civil Rights Acts of Congress Referenced in Black Americans in Congress," the Office of the Historian, 2019, history.house.gov/Exhibitions-and-Publications/BAIC/Historical-Data/Constitutional-Amendments-and-Legislation.
10. "Loving v. Virginia," Oyez, accessed on February 21, 2019, www.oyez.org/cases/1966/395.
11. "Biography," Congressman John Lewis.

CHAPTER 3: Native Americans' Civil Rights

1. "Native American History Timeline," History.com, January 15, 2019, www.history.com/topics/native-american-history/native-american-timeline.
2. "Native American History Timeline," History.com.
3. "Indian Reservations," History.com, last updated March 18, 2019, www.history.com/topics/native-american-history/indian-reservations.
4. "Voting Rights for Native Americans," Library of Congress, accessed on August 9, 2019, www.loc.gov/teachers/classroommaterials/presentationsandactivities/presentations/elections/voting-rights-native-americans.html.
5. "Voting Rights for Native Americans," Library of Congress.
6. "History of Federal Voting Rights Laws," United States Department of Justice, July 28, 2017, www.justice.gov/crt/history-federal-voting-rights-laws.
7. "Indian Civil Rights Act," WashingtonLawHelp.org, March 20, 2018, www.washingtonlawhelp.org/resource/indian-civil-rights-act.
8. "History and Culture: Indian Self Determination and Education Assistance Act," Northern Plains Reservation Aid, accessed on August 9, 2019, www.nativepartnership.org/site/PageServer?pagename=airc_hist_selfdeterminationact.
9. Adam Augustyn, "American Indian Movement," *Encyclopedia Britannica*, accessed on August 9, 2019, www.britannica.com/topic/American-Indian-Movement.
10. "Native American Activism: 1960s to Present," Zinn Education Project, 2016, www.zinnedproject.org/materials/native-american-activism-1960s-to-present/.
11. "Nov. 20, 1969: Alcatraz Occupation," Zinn Education Project, 2019, www.zinnedproject.org/news/tdih/alcatraz-occupation.

12. Moonanum James and Munro Mahtowin, "Thanksgiving: A National Day of Mourning for Indians. 1998," United American Indians of New England, 2018, www.uaine.org/default.htm.
13. "Native American Activism: 1960s to Present," Zinn Education Project, 2016, www.zinnedproject.org/materials/native-american-activism-1960s-to-present/.
14. Carly Rosenfield, "Native Americans Walk from San Francisco to Washington, D.C. for U.S. Civil Rights, 1978," Global Nonviolent Action Database, April 12, 2011, nvdatabase.swarthmore.edu/content/native-americans-walk-san-francisco-washington-dc-us-civil-rights-1978.

CHAPTER 4: Women's Civil Rights

1. "Declaration of Sentiments and Resolutions," Elizabeth Cady Stanton and Susan B Anthony Papers Project, Rutgers, August 2010, ecssba.rutgers.edu/docs/seneca.html.
2. "Women's Suffrage," History.com, last updated October 9, 2018, www.history.com/topics/womens-history/the-fight-for-womens-suffrage.
3. History, Art and Archives: United States House of Representatives, "The Women's Rights Movement: 1848-1920," the Office of the Historian, March 4, 2019, history.house.gov/Exhibitions-and-Publications/WIC/Historical-Essays/No-Lady/Womens-Rights.
4. "Timeline of Legal History of Women in the United States," National Women's History Alliance, 2019, nationalwomenshistoryalliance.org/resources/womens-rights-movement/detailed-timeline.
5. "Family and Medical Leave Act," United States Department of Labor, 2019, www.dol.gov/whd/fmla.
6. Rose Eveleth, "Forty Years Ago, Women Had a Hard Time Getting Credit Cards," Smithsonian.com, January 8, 2014, www.smithsonianmag.com/smart-news/forty-years-ago-women-had

-a-hard-time-getting-credit-cards-180949289/#ttHjuYbHxMJ6VGbW.99.

7. "TIMELINE: A History of Women in the US Military," Task & Purpose, March 8, 2017, taskandpurpose.com/timeline-history-women-us-military.
8. Meryl Davids Landau, "Birth Control in America: A Brief History of Contraception," Everyday Health, July 6, 2018, www.everydayhealth.com/birth-control/contraception-birth-control-women-america.
9. Ian Landau, "12 Key Moments in the History of Women's Health," Everyday Health, last updated May 16, 2012, www.everydayhealth.com/womens-health-pictures/key-moments-in-the-history-of-womens-health.aspx.
10. "Timeline of Legal History of Women in the United States," National Women's History Alliance.

CHAPTER 5: Gay and Transgender Civil Rights

1. Jude Sheerin, "Matthew Shepard: The Murder That Changed America," BBC, October 26, 2018, www.bbc.com/news/world-us-canada-45968606.
2. "The American Gay Rights Timeline," Infoplease.com, accessed on August 9, 2019, www.infoplease.com/us/gender-issues/american-gay-rights-movement-timeline.
3. "Stonewall Riots," History.com, August 21, 2018, www.history.com/topics/gay-rights/the-stonewall-riots.
4. "Official Biography of Harvey Milk," Milkfoundation.org, accessed on August 9, 2019, milkfoundation.org/about/harvey-milk-biography.
5. "H.R.1152 - Hate Crimes Sentencing Enhancement Act of 1993," Congress.gov, accessed on August 9, 2019, www.congress.gov/bill/103rd-congress/house-bill/1152.
6. "Hate Crime Laws," United States Department of Justice, October 15, 2018, www.justice.gov/crt/hate-crime-laws.

7. "LGBT Rights Milestones Fast Facts," CNN Library, last updated July 2, 2019, www.cnn.com/2015/06/19/us/lgbt-rights-milestones-fast-facts/index.html.
8. "Know Your Rights: Transgender People and the Law," ACLU.org, accessed on August 9, 2019, www.aclu.org/know-your-rights/transgender-people-and-law.
9. "Know Your Rights: Transgender People and the Law," ACLU.org.
10. Jey Ehrenhalt, "Trans Rights and Bathroom Access Laws: A History Explained," Teaching Tolerance, October 16, 2018, www.tolerance.org/magazine/transgender-bathroom-laws-history.
11. Adam Litptak, "Supreme Court Revives Transgender Ban for Military Service," *New York Times*, January 22, 2019, www.nytimes.com/2019/01/22/us/politics/transgender-ban-military-supreme-court.html.

CHAPTER 6: Where Are We Today?

1. "Herstory," Black Lives Matter, accessed on August 9, 2019, blacklivesmatter.com/about/herstory.
2. Maggie Fox, "Police Killings Hit People of Color Hardest, Study Finds," NBC, May 8, 2018, www.nbcnews.com/health/health-news/police-killings-hit-people-color-hardest-study-finds-n872086.
3. Kirsten Salyer, "The Racial Wage Gap Has Not Changed in 35 Years," *Time*, July 1, 2016, time.com/4390212/race-wage-gap-pew-analysis/.
4. Deborah J. Vagins, "The Simple Truth About the Gender Pay Gap," AAUW.org, 2019, www.aauw.org/research/the-simple-truth-about-the-gender-pay-gap.
5. Amanda Reed, "Walmart and Sex Discrimination," National Organization for Women, June 6, 2013, now.org/blog/walmart-and-sex-discrimination/.

6. Vanessa Romo, "Native American Tribes File Lawsuit Seeking to Invalidate Keystone XL Pipeline Permit," National Public Radio, September 10, 2018, www.npr.org/2018/09/10/646523140/native-american-tribes-file-lawsuit-seeking-to-invalidate-keystone-xl-pipeline-p.
7. Nadia Popovich, "Bears Ears National Monument Is Shrinking. Here's What Is Being Cut," *New York Times*, December 8, 2017, www.nytimes.com/interactive/2017/12/08/climate/bears-ears-monument-trump.html.
8. Hallie Detrick, "Trump Plans to Shrink Two National Monuments by up to 85%. Here's Why," *Fortune*, December 4, 2017, fortune.com/2017/12/04/donald-trump-national-monuments-bears-ears/.
9. Erin Vogel-Fox and Jessie Karangu, "Timeline: A History of LGBTQ Hurdles in Military Service," Sinclair Broadcast Group, July 26, 2017, wjla.com/news/nation-world/timeline-a-history-of-lgbtq-hurdles-in-military-service.
10. Jean Schroedel and Melissa Rogers, "What Keeps Native Americans from Voting—and What Could Change This," *Washington Post*, October 18, 2018, www.washingtonpost.com/news/monkey-cage/wp/2018/10/18/what-keeps-native-americans-from-voting-and-what-could-change-this/?utm_term=.c0109c46fcbd.
11. Susan Milligan, "States Move to Expand LGBT Protections," *US News & World Report*, February 28, 2019, www.usnews.com/news/best-states/articles/2019-02-28/states-aim-to-ban-conversion-therapy-protect-lgbtq-youth.
12. "Born Perfect: The Facts About Conversion Therapy," National Center for Lesbian Rights, accessed on August 9, 2019, www.nclrights.org/bornperfect-the-facts-about-conversion-therapy.

GLOSSARY

act A statute or law made by a legislative body such as Congress. Acts can expire or be changed more easily than the Constitution can.

amendment An article added to the Constitution that causes it to change. It is harder to amend the Constitution than it is to pass an ordinary law.

civil rights Equal rights to political and social freedoms.

Constitution The document for all legal authority in the United States.

discrimination Unjust treatment of people due to their race, religion, sex, sexual orientation, or age.

equality Having the same rights and access to resources as others do.

hate crime A crime that is motivated by a hatred of someone else's race, gender, religion, or sexual orientation.

LGBT+ An overall term for the lesbian, gay, bisexual, and transgender community.

Native Americans Groups of people who have lived in America since before European explorers and settlers arrived.

suffrage The right to vote.

transgender The state of having a gender identity that does not match one's biological sex.

FURTHER READING

BOOKS

Charleyboy, Lisa, and Mary Beth Leatherdale, eds. *#NotYourPrincess: Voices of Native American Women.* Toronto, ON, Canada: Annick Press, 2018.

Kops, Deborah. *Alice Paul and the Fight for Women's Rights: From the Vote to the Equal Rights Amendment.* Honesdale, PA: Calkins Creek, 2017.

Patillo Beals, Melba. *March Forward, Girl: From Young Warrior to Little Rock Nine.* Boston, MA: Houghton Mifflin Harcourt, 2018.

WEBSITES

ACLU: LGBTQ Youth and Schools Resource Library
www.aclu.org/library-lgbt-youth-schools-resources-and-links
This website houses a collection of resources about LGBT+ students and their rights.

Civil Rights Trail
civilrightstrail.com
Civil Rights Trail is a resource about the civil rights movement with detailed articles.

Native American Activism: 1960s to the Present
www.zinnedproject.org/materials/native-american-activism-1960s-to-present
This website provides a chronology and collection of articles detailing the current fight for Native Americans rights.

INDEX